Where Is It?

This book belongs to

_____

Where Is It?
A Language Learning Book for Wonderful Kids with Autism

PEC Books. ™
Twin Taurus Publishing ™

Copyright ©2012 Twin Taurus Publishing ™
All rights reserved under International, Pan-American, and US Copyright law.
Published by PEC BOOKS ™ and Twin Taurus Publishing ™ of South Portland, Maine, USA.

PECBooks.com
TwinTaurusPublishing.com

ISBN (10) : 1614240035
ISBN(13) : 978-1-61424-003-7

Library of Congress Control Number: 2012935152

Where Is It?

The ability to ask questions is a fundamental life skill. Asking questions not only enhances a child's learning potential, but is also critical to his or her safety and independence. Imagine living a single day without the capacity to inquire about the things and people you need. "Where is it?" is essential to communication and problem-solving skill development.

This uniquely effective picture book is the cooperative effort of Parents, Experts, and Children (PEC). It is designed to teach wonderful kids with developmental delays like Autism Spectrum Disorders by minimizing learning interference elements and making use of the extraordinary gifts so many challenged children possess. Repeated readings help demonstrate the purpose of asking questions and encourage children to ask independently. Some objects appear in the pictures scenes, but are not mentioned in the text. These objects offer additional opportunities for children and adults to practice asking and answering.

Books by
Parents, Experts, and Children

PEC Books are learning tools created by Parents, Experts, and Children. PEC projects reflect the experience, research, and wisdom of those most familiar with the challenges and opportunities that come with early childhood education and special needs. PEC Books are specifically designed for use with children facing developmental disabilities, but are beneficial to children of all abilities. Parents and educators can increase the effectiveness of this book by clearly demonstrating the use of questions in casual, real-life situations.

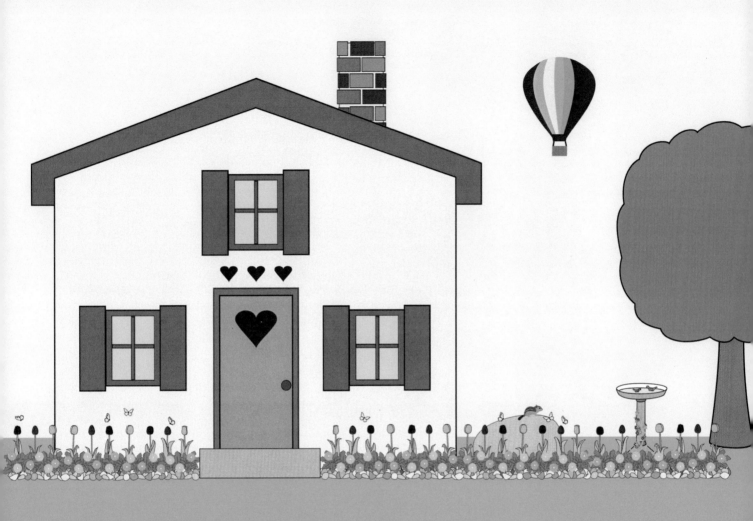

Where are we?

We're **in** the yard.

Where is the sail boat?

It's **on** the garage.

Where is the car?

It's **in** the garage.

Where is the dog?

It's **under** the tree.

Where is the cat?

It's **on** the fence.

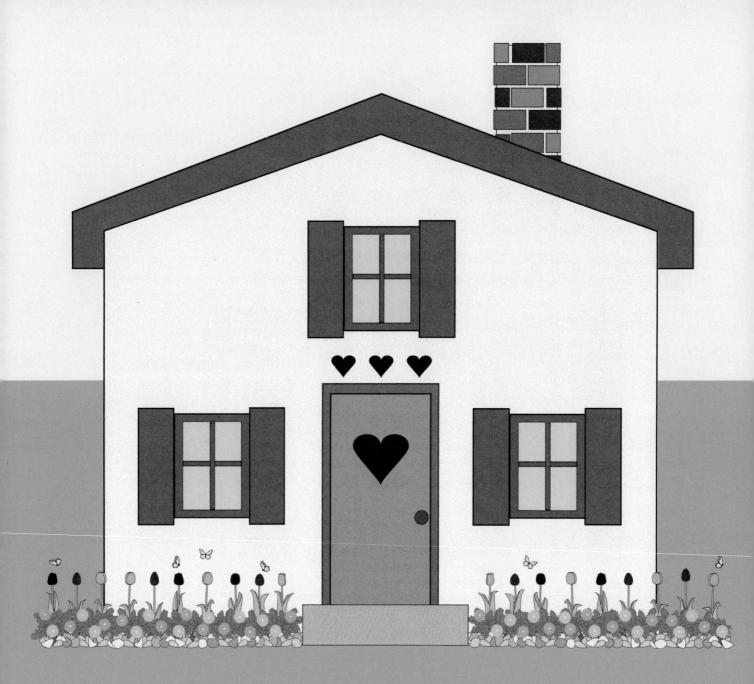

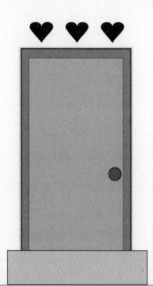

Where are the small hearts?

They're **over** the door.

Where is the big heart?

It's **on** the door.

Where are we?

We're **in** the garden.

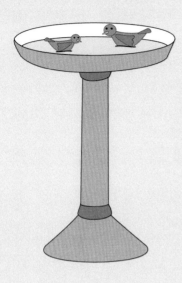

Where are the birds?

They're **in** the bird bath.

Where are the flowers?

They're **under** the bird bath.

Where is the bee?

It's **on** the flower.

Where are the rocks?

They're **under** the flowers.

Where are the butterflies?

They're **over** the flowers.

Where is the chipmunk?

It's **on** the rock.

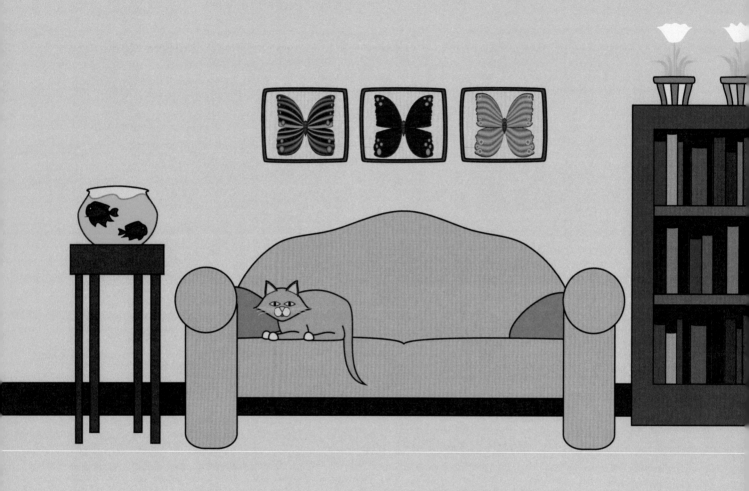

Where are we?

We're **in** the living room.

Where is the cat?

It's **on** the couch.

Where are the butterflies?

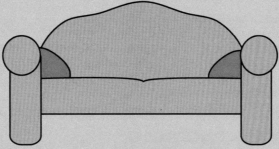

They're **over** the couch.

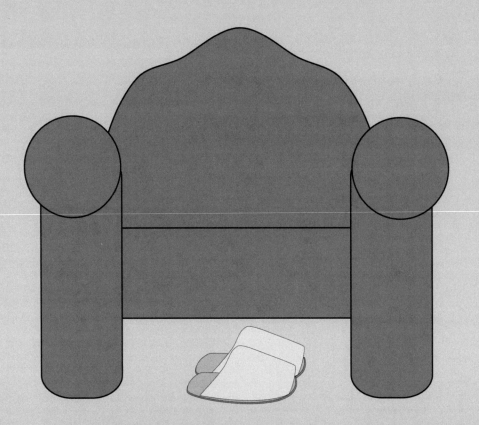

Where is the tree?

It's **over** the chair.

Where are the slippers?

They're **under** the chair.

Where is the lamp?

It's **on** the table.

Where is the dog?

It's **under** the table.

Where are the flowers?

They're **on** the bookcase.

Where are the books?

They're **in** the bookcase.

Where are we?

We're **in** the bedroom.

Where is the teddy bear?

It's **on** the bed.

Where are the stars?

They're **over** the bed.

Where are the robots?

They're **on** the shelf.

Where are the toys?

They're **in** the toy box.

Where is the rainbow?

It's **over** the desk.

Where are the crayons?

They're **on** the desk.

A note of thanks...

To the parents, experts, and children who have contributed to this project both directly and indirectly, a tremendous debt of gratitude is owed. These books would not be possible without your interest, ideas, time, and effort.

To the heroic women and men who devote their lives and careers to the advancement of children with developmental challenges, no words could ever convey our appreciation. Your dedication and constant efforts make a very real difference in the fight to save children whose gifts might otherwise be overlooked and whose potential would likely be discarded. Thank you.

Made in the USA
Lexington, KY
05 July 2018